George Washington

YOUNG LEADER

George Washington

YOUNG LEADER

by Laurence Santrey
illustrated by William Ostrowsey

Troll Associates

Library of Congress Cataloging in Publication Data

Santrey, Laurence.
  George Washington, young leader.

    Summary: Traces the life of the first president of
the United States from his boyhood years at Mount
Vernon to his adult years.
      1. Washington, George, 1732-1799—Childhood and youth
—Juvenile literature.   2. Presidents—United States—
Biography—Juvenile literature.   [1. Washington,
George, 1732-1799.   2. Presidents]   I. Ostrowsey,
William, ill.   II. Title.
E312.2.S256   973.4′1′0973 [B] [92]   81-23150
ISBN 0-89375-758-6   AACR2
ISBN 0-89375-759-4 (pbk.)

George Washington

YOUNG LEADER

"Look there, George," Augustine Washington said. He pointed to a clump of bushes.

"What is it, Papa?" the three-year-old boy asked.

"A red fox," the tall man whispered. "Now stay very still, and maybe he'll come out into the open."

Father and son watched as the furry, red animal crept out and stood still, sniffing the air.

The little boy tried to stop himself, but couldn't. He giggled merrily. The startled fox ran off as fast as it could. George looked up at his father, who smiled and put a loving hand on the boy's shoulder.

Little George Washington was excited by everything about his new home. It stood on a hill that looked out over the beautiful, mile-wide Potomac River. The place, called Little Hunting Creek, was a perfect world for the sturdy, adventurous boy. There were woods where he could roam for hours, looking for all kinds of animals and birds. Not far away was the creek, a bubbling stream filled with fish just waiting to be caught. Virginia in the summer of 1735 was a fine place to be growing up.

Three years earlier, when George was born, on February 22, 1732, Augustine and Mary Washington lived on a farm in Pope's Creek, Virginia. George's great-grandfather, John, had settled on this land in 1658, after marrying Anne Pope. In time, the Washingtons grew rich and owned many thousands of acres in Virginia. But it all had started with the 700-acre property on Pope's Creek.

Year after year, the Pope's Creek land produced fine crops. But by 1735, the once-rich soil was worn out. The harvest was getting smaller and smaller. It was, as Augustine Washington said, "time to let this land rest awhile. Little Hunting Creek has never been farmed. That's where we shall move."

The new, two-story home of the Washingtons was small and simple. There was a hall that ran down the center of the house, from the front door to the back door. On each side of this hall were two rooms. Upstairs, there was another hall and four more rooms. All of the upstairs rooms were bedrooms. One was for Mr. and Mrs. Washington. One was a bedroom for their sons, another was for their daughters. The fourth bedroom was for guests or grandparents.

Downstairs, there was a dining room, a den, and two parlors. An eight-room house like this sounds large and grand, but it wasn't. The rooms were very small, and there were no closets in the house. Everything had to be kept in big, wooden chests standing in the rooms. Also, most families were large in those days. So, if there were four brothers, four beds had to be squeezed into one tiny room. If there were three or four or eight sisters—no matter how many—they would all sleep in the girls' room. And if there were more people than beds in a room, two or three of the boys or girls had to share a bed.

Every room had a fireplace, and a space for stacking wood. To crowd things even more, a colonial house had lots of chairs, a couple of couches for extra guests to sleep on, tables, and other pieces of furniture.

14

Around the main house stood several one-room buildings. There was a bake-house, with a big oven for making bread and cakes. There was a kitchen, where food was cooked for everyone—family, guests, and workers—living on the farm. The kitchen was separate from the main house because it was smoky, greasy, and smelly. It had a hearth so big that a whole suckling pig and huge iron pots of beans and soups could all be cooked at the same time. It was good, healthful food—but by the time it made the trip from the kitchen house to the main house (especially in winter), it was usually cold.

The other buildings near the main house were storage sheds, barns, stables, a dairy, a smokehouse for meats, a blacksmith's forge, a carpenter's shop, and an outhouse.

The Washingtons lived at Little Hunting Creek for three years. It was a happy, peaceful place to be. George spent his days learning to ride a pony, and playing with his little sister, Betty, and baby brother, Samuel. There were no neighbors for miles around, so George had no other playmates. And, of course, there was no school. Which is one of the reasons the Washingtons moved again, when George was six.

Ferry Farm, their new home, was right across the Rappahannock River from the small town of Fredericksburg, Virginia. The farm was named for a ferry that went back and forth across the river. The Washingtons owned the ferry and collected a fee from every person who used it.

When George was seven he started going to a one-room schoolhouse in Fredericksburg. It was run by Reverend James Marye. Every day George rode the ferry across the river to get to school. There the children learned reading, writing, and simple arithmetic.

Young George liked arithmetic best of all. The numbers made sense to him. Two and two always added up to four. And six times five was always thirty.

Spelling was something else. George thought it was silly that the word "through" didn't rhyme with the word "rough." He believed that "through" should be spelled "threw," and that "rough" should be spelled "ruff."

"Words should look the way they sound," he told Reverend Marye.

The teacher smiled. Then he looked at the words George had printed on his slate and shook his head. Fourteen of the twenty words were spelled wrong. "There is sense in what you say, George," he said. "But you must learn to spell as we all do. If you wish to be considered a gentleman, you must spell correctly and write with a fine, clear hand."

George very much wanted to be a gentleman. His half-brothers, Lawrence and Austin (sons of Mr. Washington and his first wife, Jane Butler), had years of schooling in England. Now George was setting out to be just as much the gentleman as they were. And if spelling and clear penmanship were part of it, then he would work hard to improve his. He practiced his writing over and over, trying to make the letters round and smooth and easy to read.

As for spelling, George followed Reverend Marye's suggestion: "Seek the word you need in the books your father has in his library. Read and try to remember everything you read."

When George could not spell a word, he began looking through his father's books. Sometimes he had to read for hours before the word turned up. There were no dictionaries when George was a boy, so he had no easy way to look up the spelling or meaning of a word.

George wanted people to admire his good manners, too. So he again turned to books for help. From one book he copied out many rules of good manners, and he tried to live by these rules.

But George wasn't all book-learning and good manners. He also was a strong, healthy boy who was excellent at outdoor sports. From the day he was first put on a pony, George loved to ride. He rode with a saddle or bareback. No horse was too spirited for him, no stream too wide to jump, no fence too high to clear. Many years later, Thomas Jefferson called George Washington the finest horseman he had ever seen.

Young George was a fine marksman, too. Learning to shoot wasn't just for fun. The wild animals George and his father bagged were used as food. There were deer and duck, squirrels, rabbits, and grouse. George also practiced marksmanship with his friends. They would set up a row of ten pine cones on a log. The boy who hit the most cones with ten shots was the winner of the shoot. George won most of the time.

Whatever sport George tried, he did well. He was the best wrestler of any boy his age, and the fastest runner. When it came to "throwing the bar"—which was like throwing the javelin today—and pole vaulting, not even the older boys could beat George.

When George was ten something new was added to his world. His half-brothers, Lawrence and Austin, returned home. Austin arrived from England, where he had completed his schooling.

Lawrence, a captain in the American Regiment under Admiral Edward Vernon, had served valiantly in the Caribbean against Spanish pirates. The gallant officer, with his gleaming medals and sword, was George's hero. The boy would hang over his brother's chair wherever he sat, and would follow him from room to room.

"Tell me, Lawrence, is it very exciting to stand on the deck of a warship when the wind is sharp and the waves are high?" George asked, his eyes aglow.

Lawrence laughed good-naturedly. "Aye, exciting it is, little brother. If you fancy being wet to the skin, bone-chilled, and sick to your stomach half the time." The broad-shouldered officer tapped the ashes from his pipe into the fireplace, then put an arm around George's shoulder. "I think your mother will not want you to go to sea," Lawrence continued. "And you must forgive me if I take her side in this matter."

George sighed. "It seems, then, that I shall forever live a dull life," he said. "And I wished so hard to travel everywhere and win glory in battle."

"You'll find glory enough without setting foot on the deck of a man-of-war," Lawrence said. "You'll serve your time in the Virginia Militia, then take your place among the leaders of this colony."

George shrugged. "That does not sound a hero's life to me," he muttered.

"Ah, well," Lawrence said, "perhaps not. But who can tell what the future will bring?"

George was disappointed. But he couldn't brood about it for long. Not with Lawrence taking him out riding and hunting and fishing. And not with Austin teaching him the business of running a farm. George didn't mind this at all, since much of it had to do with numbers.

Such as, the number of acres to be plowed. And how many pounds of tobacco an acre would yield. And taxes. And profits. And the cost of food and clothing. George learned his lessons well. If he was going to have to be a Virginia planter, he wanted to be the best one possible.

To learn even more, George was sent to visit relatives in all parts of the colony. His school days were over. They were replaced by travel, new places, new people—seeing the world away from Ferry Farm.

In the spring of 1743, when he was eleven, George was staying with some cousins in the Chotank district of the Potomac. This was great hunting country, and the young people were out riding in the woods and fields every day. Then one day a messenger arrived with word that Mr. Washington was gravely ill. George was to return home immediately.

George galloped home, without stopping. On his arrival he found his father near death. The entire family had gathered around him. Mr. Washington spoke to his children, one by one, and then to his wife. A few minutes later he was dead.

Augustine Washington left a great deal of property to his family. Lawrence, the oldest son, was given the estate on Little Hunting Creek. Austin, next oldest, got the farm at Pope's Creek and twenty-five head of cattle. George got Ferry Farm. Samuel, John, and Charles— George's younger brothers—received small farms. Betty, the only daughter, was given a large sum of money, furniture, and jewelry.

Mrs. Washington was left in charge of the property willed to George, his sister, and his younger brothers. She would look after the farms until they were old enough to manage by themselves.

Soon after his father's death, George went to stay with Lawrence at Little Hunting Creek. The eleven-year-old still had quite a lot to learn about owning and running a farm, and Lawrence offered to teach him.

It wasn't just paperwork. Lawrence also took him out into the fields, showing him how tobacco was planted, tended, and harvested. He introduced George to all the important people living nearby. He took the boy on fox hunts, to dances and dinner parties, to the horse races, and to other social events.

George loved the life he was living now. And he admired Lawrence, who was almost like a father to him. He also got along very well with Anne Fairfax Washington, Lawrence's new bride. She was the big sister George had never had. She taught him how to dance, talk to young ladies, and dress pleasingly. Learning to be a gentleman mattered as much to George as learning to be a landowner.

The sounds of hammers and saws filled the air all day long at Little Hunting Creek. George watched the workers as they enlarged Lawrence's house. Soon it was a very grand mansion. No longer was it called Little Hunting Creek. The new name was Mount Vernon, in honor of Admiral Vernon, under whom Lawrence had served in the regiment.

Years later, after Lawrence died, Mount Vernon became George's property. He returned to his deeply loved home as often as possible. But it wasn't until the last years of his life that he could spend much time there. Only after serving his country as Commander-in-Chief of the Continental Army and as its first President was George finally free to enjoy the beauty and peace of Mount Vernon.

During George's early teen years, he was busy all the time. When he wasn't at Mount Vernon with Lawrence, he would stay for a few weeks with Austin. Then he would spend two or three months with his mother, or he would visit other relatives in different parts of Virginia. Traveling from place to place on horseback was an education in itself. It gave George an understanding of the land and people that he never could have gained from books. And these lessons, once learned, were never forgotten.

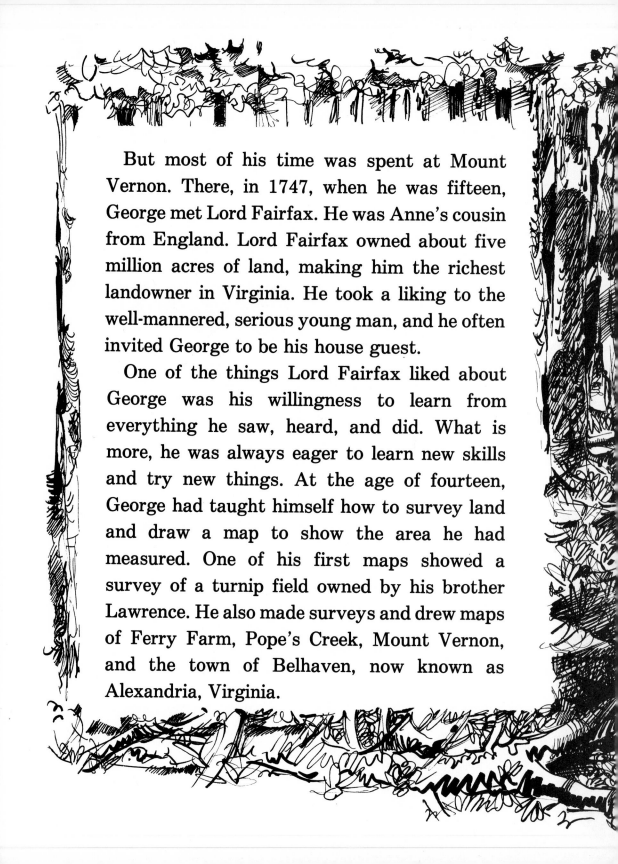

But most of his time was spent at Mount Vernon. There, in 1747, when he was fifteen, George met Lord Fairfax. He was Anne's cousin from England. Lord Fairfax owned about five million acres of land, making him the richest landowner in Virginia. He took a liking to the well-mannered, serious young man, and he often invited George to be his house guest.

One of the things Lord Fairfax liked about George was his willingness to learn from everything he saw, heard, and did. What is more, he was always eager to learn new skills and try new things. At the age of fourteen, George had taught himself how to survey land and draw a map to show the area he had measured. One of his first maps showed a survey of a turnip field owned by his brother Lawrence. He also made surveys and drew maps of Ferry Farm, Pope's Creek, Mount Vernon, and the town of Belhaven, now known as Alexandria, Virginia.

When Lord Fairfax learned of George's surveying skill, he asked the teenager to visit him. At dinner, the Englishman questioned George more closely about surveying. George told how he had learned to use his father's old surveying tools, and how much he liked doing the work.

"Well, then, George," Lord Fairfax said, "I have an idea. It can bring rewards to both of us. My landholdings in this country are not yet charted, and I am sending my cousin, George William, and a surveyor to accomplish this task. But one surveyor is not enough. Would you, my boy, care to join them in this venture?"

"Yes, sir!" George said excitedly. "When do we leave?"

"My, what an eager lad you are," Lord Fairfax said, chuckling. "And you've not even heard the wages. You shall be paid a doubloon a day. Does that please you?"

"Both the wage and work please me, sir," George said.

Lawrence was delighted at the news. George would have his first chance to see the wilderness, have a job, and earn good pay (a doubloon then was worth about twenty dollars today).

The survey party left on March 11, 1748. Spring was in the air. On that first day, they covered forty miles before making camp. In the thirty-three days that followed, sixteen-year-old George had the time of his life. He kept the field notes for the survey, swam horses over the south branch of the Potomac, paddled thirty-eight miles in a canoe in one day, saw his first rattlesnake, shot a twenty-pound wild turkey, and ate it for dinner.

One of the highlights of the journey over the Blue Ridge Mountains and through the Shenandoah Valley was, in George's words, "meeting thirty Indians." The two groups camped close together, and that night George watched with fascination as the Indians did a war dance.

All that George heard and saw and did on this trip changed him. In a way, the boy who left Mount Vernon was a budding English gentleman, and the young man who came back was an American. In those thirty-three days, George discovered forests and rivers and mountains—a new world that reached farther west than the eye could see. He had felt the frontier, and he would never be the same again.

It was this spirit that filled George Washington until the day he died, on December 14, 1799. It inspired him to battle heroically for his native land during the American Revolution. He became a symbol of strength, honor, and unshakable faith in freedom. No man was better suited to be the nation's first President. And no man is remembered with more respect.